Couples

A hot little book about us.

haVoc
PUBLISHING

©1997 Havoc Publishing

ISBN 0-7416-9983-4

Published and created by Havoc Publishing

San Diego, California

First Printing, May 1997

Designed by Juddesign

Some images ©1997 PhotoDisc, Inc.

Made in Korea

Please write to us for more information on our

Havoc Publishing Record Books and Products.

HAVOC PUBLISHING
9808 Waples Street,
San Diego, CA 92121

www.havocpub.com

Couples

A hot little book about us

A record book for

&

Contents

All About Us

In the Beginning & Our First Date

Photographs

Our First Kiss

Our Most Exciting & Miserable Dates

I Knew I Loved You When & Saying the "L" Word

Meeting the Parents

Trips

Photographs

Tokens of Affection

Celebrations

The First Item We Purchased Together

Photographs

Our Differences & Similarities

Best Personality Traits & Physical Attributes

Contents

Memorabilia

Affectionate Pet Names

Love Notes

Things We Should Just Do Alone

Favorite Rainy Day Activities

The Best of Times...

Feast on This

Favorite Recipe & Menu

Song and Dance

Nights At Home

Out on the Town

Programs & Ticket Stubs

What I've Always Wanted to Tell You

Photographs

Our Future

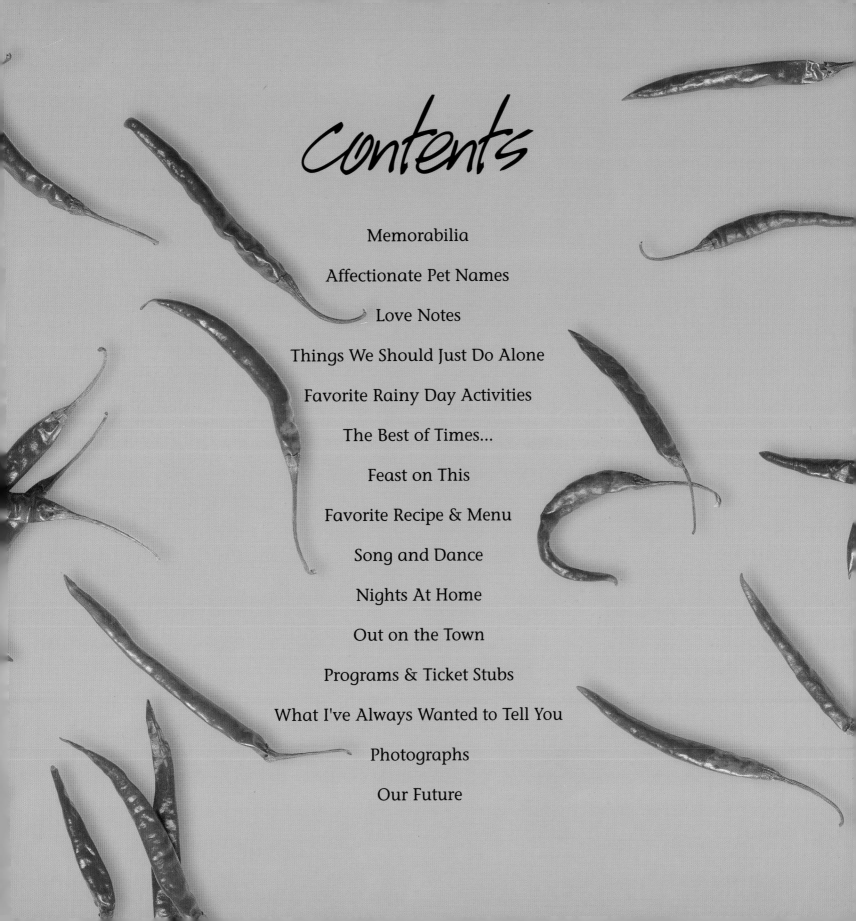

All About Us

Her career _____

His career _____

Her hobbies and interests _____

His hobbies and interests _____

How she relaxes _____

How he relaxes _____

In The Beginning

How we met

_____

_____

_____

Where we met

_____

_____

What attracted us to each other

_____

_____

First impressions

_____

_____

How long before we went out

_____

_____

Our First Date

When _____

Where we went _____

Who asked whom _____

Best part of the date _____

_____

_____

We were most nervous about _____

_____

Who called whom first _____

Photograph

Photograph

Our First Kiss

When _____

Where _____

Who kissed whom _____

We'll always remember _____

_____

_____

_____

_____

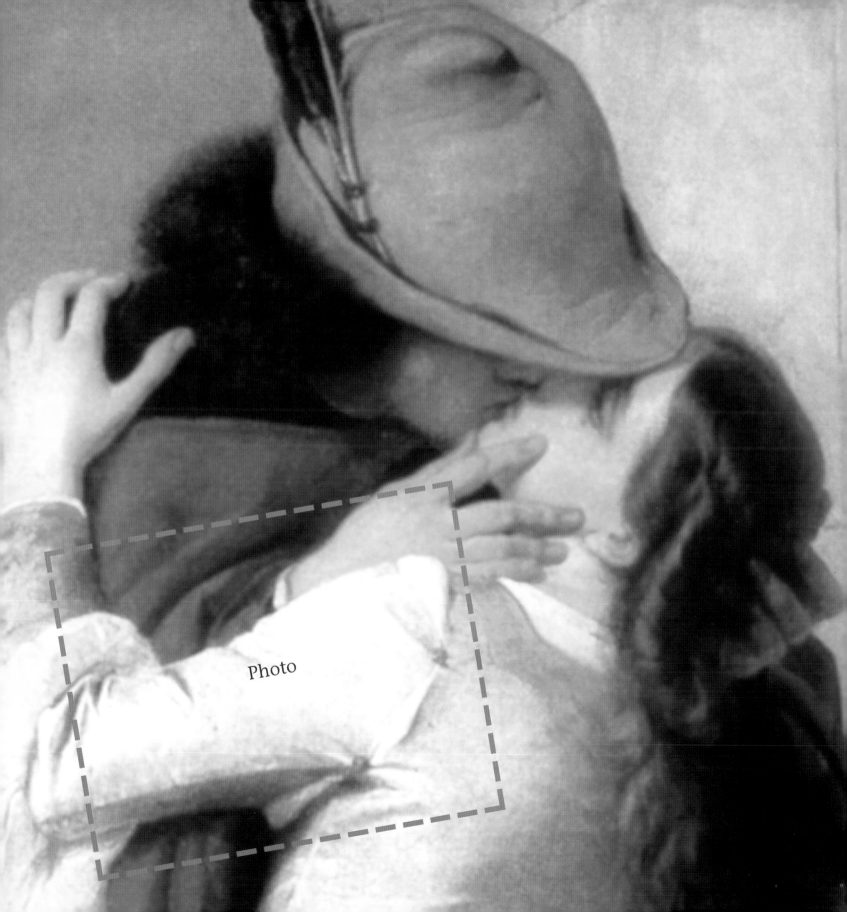

Photo

Our Most Exciting Date

When _____

Where we went _____

What made it so exciting _____

_____

_____

_____

_____

_____

_____

Our Most
Miserable Date

When _____

Where we went _____

Why it was so miserable _____

_____

_____

_____

_____

_____

I Knew I Loved You When...

Saying The "L" Word

Who said it first _____

When _____

Where _____

His reaction _____

_____

Her reaction _____

_____

Dad picture here

Mom picture here

Meeting The Parents

His

When _____

Where _____

_____

What we did _____

_____

_____

How it went _____

_____

_____

_____

Hers

When _____

Where _____

_____

What we did _____

_____

_____

How it went _____

_____

_____

Our First Trip

When

Where

What happened along the way

Our Favorite Trip

When

Where

What we did

Our Most Romantic Getaway

When _____

Where _____

Why it was so romantic _____

_____

_____

_____

_____

_____

_____

_____

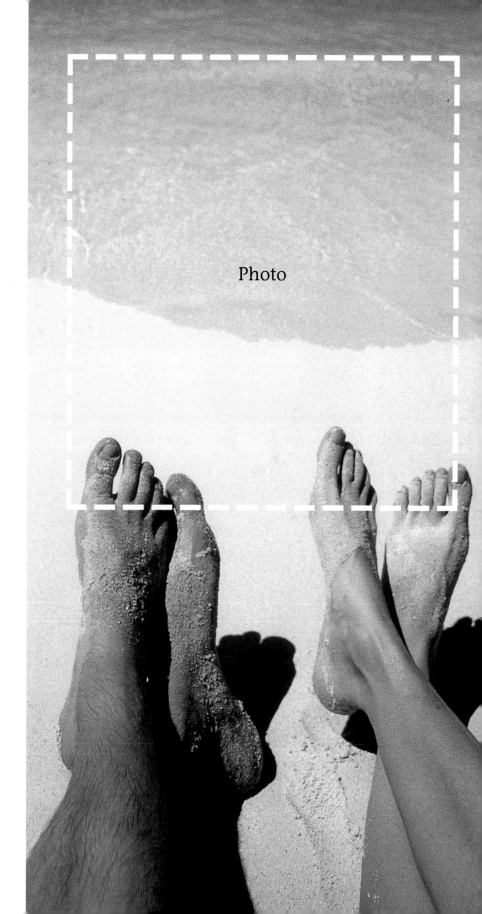

Photo

Photograph

Photograph

Tokens of Affection

The first gift he gave her

_____

_____

The first gift she gave him

_____

_____

His favorite gift

_____

Why

_____

_____

_____

Her favorite gift

_____

Why

_____

_____

_____

The most romantic gift

_____

_____

The most romantic gift

_____

_____

Celebrations

His birthday

Holidays

Her birthday

Other special events

Anniversaries

How we spend them

Photo

The First Item We Purchased Together

Item _____

When _____

Where _____

How much _____

Reason _____

_____

_____

Our
Differences

Our
Similarities

_____
_____
_____
_____
_____
_____
_____
_____
_____

What he loves most about her

_____

_____

_____

_____

Best Personality Traits

What she loves most about him

_____

_____

_____

_____

His _____

_____

_____

_____

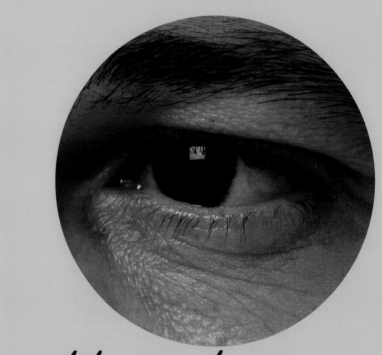

Best Physical Attributes

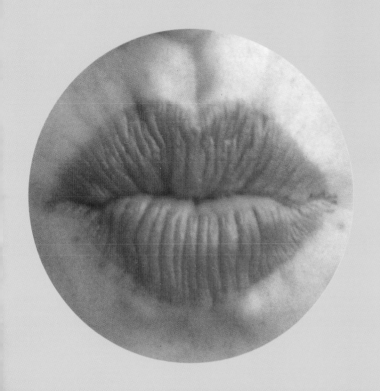

Hers _____

_____

_____

_____

_____

_____

Memorabilia

Memorabilia

Affectionate Pet Names

honey

She sometimes calls him

He sometimes calls her

sweetie

sugar

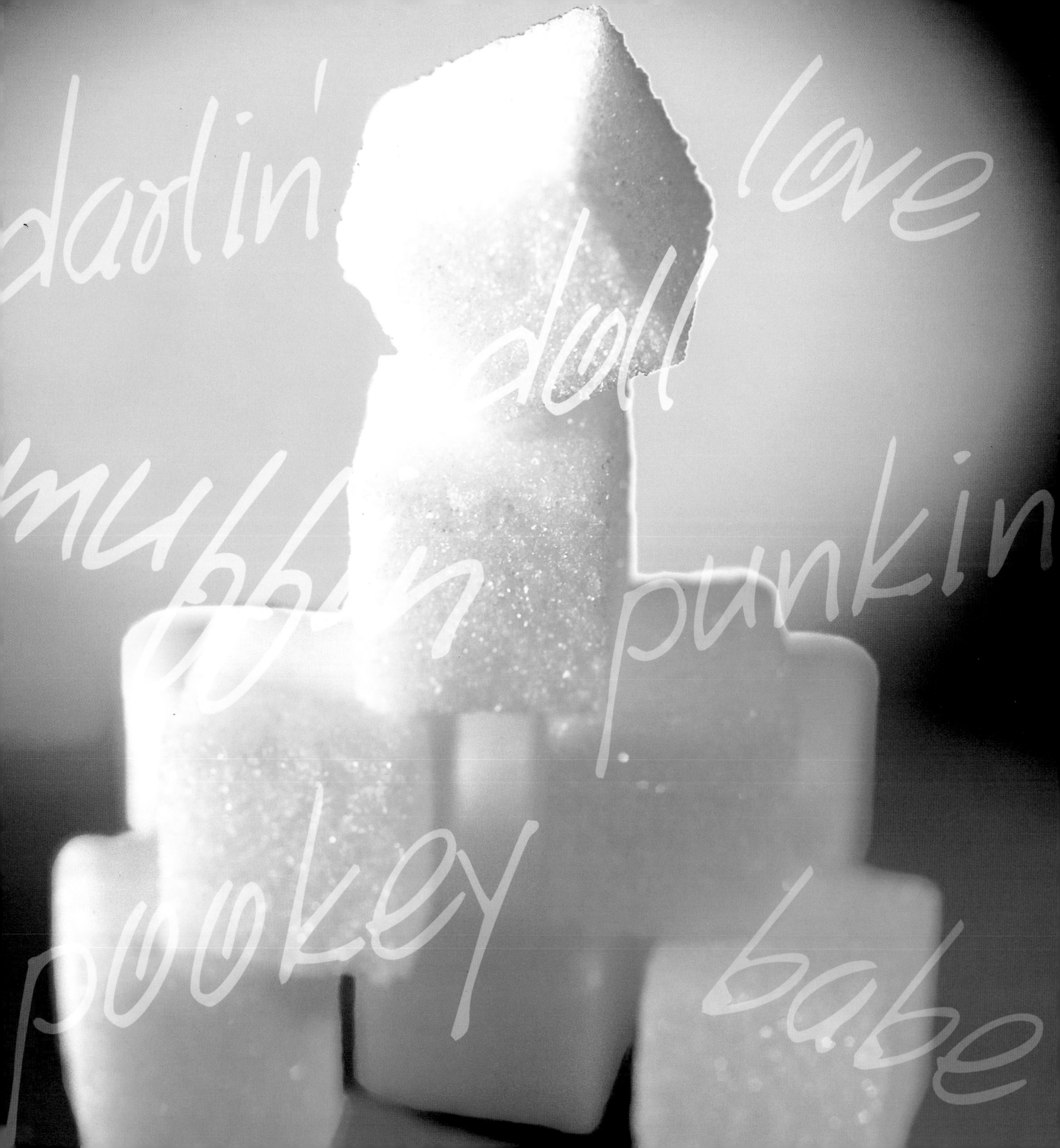
darlin'
love
doll
muffin
punkin
pookey
babe

Love Notes

Things We Should Just Do Alone

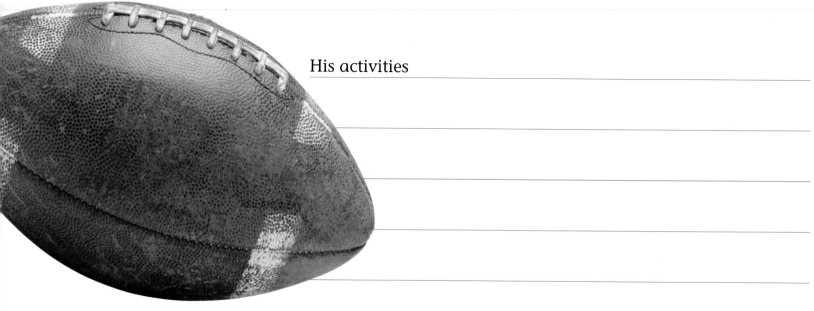

His activities

Her activities

Favorite Ways To Spend Time Together

_____

_____

_____

_____

_____

_____

_____

_____

_____

_____

Favorite Rainy Day Activities

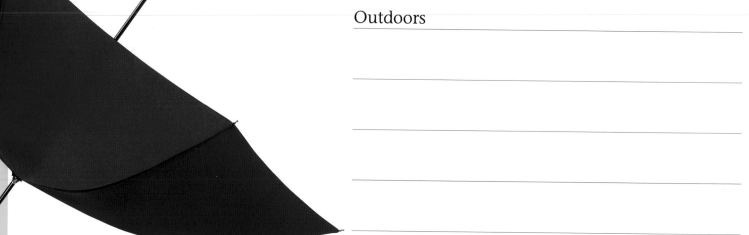

Outdoors
_____
_____
_____
_____

Indoors
_____
_____
_____
_____

The Best of Times...

The Worst of Times

Feast On This

Favorite meal

First meal he cooked for her

First meal she cooked for him

Favorite dessert

Foods he introduced to her

Foods she introduced to him

Favorite Recipe

Favorite Menu

Song and Dance

Our song _____

Why _____

_____

Our first dance _____

When _____

Where _____

Song _____

His favorite group _____

Her favorite group _____

Music she introduced to him _____

Music he introduced to her _____

_____

_____

_____

_____

Nights At Home

Our favorite activities

Our favorite meals

Our Favorite Rentals

Our favorite treats

Out On The Town

Our favorite activities

Our favorite restaurants

Our favorite dance clubs

Our favorite theatres

Our favorite plays/musicals

New places he introduced to her

New places she introduced to him

Ticket Stubs

what I've

Always Wanted
To Tell You

Photograph

Our Future

What he wishes for

_____

_____

_____

_____

_____

_____

_____

_____

What she wishes for

_____

_____

_____

_____

_____

_____

_____

Available Record Books from Havoc

Animal Antics - Cats

Animal Antics - Dogs

Couples

Girlfriends

Golf

Grandmother

Our Honeymoon

Mom

Sisters

Tying the Knot

Traveling Adventures

Please write to us with your ideas for additional
Havoc Publishing Record Books and Products

HAVOC PUBLISHING
9808 Waples Street,
San Diego, CA 92121